W9-BBM-993

781.64
KEN

Kenney, Karen Latchana
Cool reggae music : create
& . . .

$18.95
BC#32457105001105

DATE DUE	BORROWER'S NAME
	Eduardo

781.64   BC#32457105001105 $18.95
KEN   Kenney, Karen Latchana
             Cool reggae music : create
             & . . .

Morrill ES
Chicago Public Schools
6011 S Rockwell St.
Chicago, IL 60629

Cool REGGAE MUSIC

MUSIC

Create & Appreciate What Makes Music Great!

Karen Latchana Kenney

ABDO Publishing Company

Visit us at www.abdopublishing.com

Published by ABDO Publishing Company, 8000 West 78th Street, Edina, Minnesota 55439. Copyright © 2008 by Abdo Consulting Group, Inc. International copyrights reserved in all countries. No part of this book may be reproduced in any form without written permission from the publisher. The Checkerboard Library™ is a trademark and logo of ABDO Publishing Company.

Printed in the United States.

Design and Production: Mighty Media, Inc.
Photo Credits: Anders Hanson, Photodisc, Shutterstock
Series Editor: Pam Price

The following manufacturers/names appearing in this book are trademarks:
Maxwell House®, Stanley®

Library of Congress Cataloging-in-Publication Data

Kenney, Karen Latchana.
  Cool reggae music : create & appreciate what makes music great! / Karen Latchana Kenney.
      p. cm. -- (Cool music)
  Includes index.
  ISBN 978-1-59928-973-1
  1. Reggae music--History and criticism--Juvenile literature. 2. Reggae music--Instruction and study--Juvenile. I. Title.

  ML3532.K46 2008
  781.646--dc22
                              2007038997

Note to Adult Helpers

Some activities in this book require the help of an adult. An adult should closely monitor any use of a sharp object, such as a utility knife, or perform that task for the child.

Contents

The Music Around You

Did you ever get a song stuck in your head? Maybe you just couldn't help singing it out loud. Sometimes a song reminds you of a day with your friends or a fun vacation. Other times a tune may stay in your mind just because you like it so much. Listening to music can be fun and memorable for everyone.

We hear music everywhere we go. Music is played on television shows and commercials. There are even television stations dedicated to music.

Most radio stations play one type, or **genre**, of music. Some play only country music. Others play just classical music. Still others play a mixture of different kinds of rock music. Just pick a kind of music that you like, and you will find a radio station that plays it!

The different genres of music have many things in common, though. They all use instruments. Some instruments are played in many different types of music. The differences are in the ways instruments are played. For example, the drumbeats are different in various music genres.

Some kinds of music have **lyrics** that are sung by singers. Did you know that the human voice is often referred to as an instrument?

Playing music can be as fun as listening to it! Every person can play a part in a song. You can start with something simple, such as a tambourine. You could then work your way up to a more difficult instrument, such as a drum set. Remember, every great musician was once a beginner. It takes practice and time to learn how to play an instrument.

With music, one of the most important things is to have fun! You can dance to it, play it, or listen to it. Find your own musical style and make it your own!

A Mini Musical Glossary

classical music – a type of music from Europe that began centuries ago as the first written church music. Today it includes operas and music played by orchestras.

country music – a style of music that came from the rural parts of the southern United States. It is based on folk, gospel, and blues music.

hip-hop music – a style of music originally from New York City in which someone raps lyrics while a DJ plays or creates an instrumental track.

Latin music – a genre of music that includes several styles of music from Latin America. It is influenced by African, European, and native musical styles. Songs may be sung in Spanish, Portuguese, or Latin-based Creole.

reggae music – a type of music that came from Jamaica in the 1960s. It is based on African and Caribbean music and American **rhythm and blues**.

rock music – a genre of music that became popular in the 1950s. It is based on country music and rhythm-and-blues styles.

The Reggae Story

The small Caribbean island of Jamaica produced the big sound of reggae music. This music had many influences. It came from African folk music and from American **rhythm and blues** and **jazz**. Jamaicans built on these influences and made a unique sound. This sound won over the world.

Mid-1600s to mid-1800s. Jamaica became the property of Great Britain. During this time, hundreds of thousands of African slaves were brought to Jamaica. Many stayed to work on the sugar plantations when slavery was abolished in 1838. Jamaica now had a large population of African people.

1930s. The Rastafarian movement began in Jamaica. This movement promoted black pride, love, and self-respect. Many poor black people began to follow **Rastafarianism**. They were called Rastas. They grew their hair into **dreadlocks** and wore the colors red, gold, and green. Rasta music, using African drumming rhythms, was developed.

1900

1925

1950

1880s. The Alpha Boys' School was formed in Kingston, Jamaica. In the 1940s, this Catholic school began training boys to play brass instruments. Many famous brass players have come from this school. They include Rico Rodriguez and Don Drummond.

Early 1950s. American rhythm and blues (R & B) became very popular in Jamaica. Jamaicans heard this music on sound systems. Sound systems are traveling music parties. A sound-system man plays records in outdoor areas set up with large speakers and **turntables**. Some popular sound-system men are Duke Reid, Sir Coxone Dodd, and Prince Buster.

Late 1950s. Ska music developed in Jamaica. Ska was a Jamaican version of R & B and jazz, mixed with a type of Jamaican folk music called mento. It was heavily instrumental. Sound-system men started recording studios and began to record ska. The Skatalites and Desmond Dekker were masters of the ska sound.

Late 1960s to early 1970s. Reggae music was born. It had a slower rhythm than rock steady. This music emphasized the electric bass and electric organ. Jamaican music no longer sounded like a copy of American music. Reggae had a uniquely Jamaican sound.

1980s to 1990s. Dancehall music developed from reggae. It had a faster beat, and a DJ or a lyricist rapped or sang over the music. King Jammy, Shaggy, and Buju Banton helped make this dance music popular.

2000

1975

Mid to late 1960s. A new music called rock steady emerged. It was slower than ska and emphasized harmonizing vocals. Its **lyrics** told serious thoughts about life and politics. Toots and the Maytals and the Paragons are important rock steady groups.

1970s to 1980s. Reggae took on the Rastafarian message and became roots reggae. Messages of love, peace, and political protest were laced through the lyrics of this music. These messages helped make reggae popular around the world. Bob Marley and the Wailers and Burning Spear became international stars of this music.

Today. Reggae music is played all over the world. There are yearly reggae festivals in the United States, Canada, Europe, and the Caribbean. Bands from different countries play their own versions of reggae music. The swinging beat, serious lyrics, and upbeat sound have spread this music from Jamaica to the rest of the world.

What Is Reggae Music?

Reggae has a unique sound. It is rhythmic and soulful and has a hypnotic quality. Reggae music has some basic elements. What are these elements? What gives them a reggae sound?

Reggae Rhythm

Reggae rhythm comes not only from **percussion** instruments but also from guitar chords and a bass **riff**, or tune. The reggae beat usually has a 4/4 rhythm. This means that the beats are counted out in sets of four.

The base riff forms the foundation of the song. The riff is the lowest sound and is repeated over and over. Percussion is added to accompany the riff. Percussion is usually played on a drum set. But it can also be played on bongos or other types of drums or shakers.

Guitar chords are added. They emphasize the second and fourth beats. These rhythmic chords are usually played twice and quickly. This gives the music a bouncing effect. This is probably the most recognizable sound of reggae music.

CLEF NOTES

Ska bands have very different setups from reggae bands. They usually have 10 to 20 members. Ska bands have large horn sections and play in a big-band **jazz** style.

Lyrics

Reggae **lyrics** range from serious to light topics. Many song lyrics mention poverty and describe difficult lives. Other lyrics describe happy times and dancing. Some promote love. Many times, reggae lyrics use language from Jamaican culture.

Who's Who in a Reggae Group

A typical reggae group has five to six members. The lead singer sings the lyrics and may also play an instrument.

The percussionist plays a drum kit, bongos, cowbells, claves, or shakers. The bassist plays the electric bass guitar. The rhythm guitarist plays chords on an electric guitar. The organist may also play chords on an electric organ or keyboard. The lead guitarist plays the electric guitar.

Sometimes woodwind and brass instruments are added. They include saxophones, trombones, and trumpets.

PERCUSSIONIST

BASSIST

RHYTHM GUITAR

ORGANIST

LEAD GUITAR

SINGER

Reggae Instruments

Reggae bands have some basic instruments that make up the reggae sound. Other instruments are also added to create a different sound.

Basic Reggae Instruments

drum kit

lead guitar and rhythm guitar

bass guitar

keyboard

Additional Instruments

bongos

claves

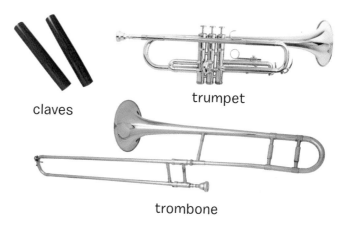

trumpet

trombone

shaker

cowbell

saxophone

Reggae Tools

Bands also need some tools that are not instruments to make reggae music. Without these tools, you wouldn't be able to hear that reggae sound.

Microphones. Microphones change the sounds from the singer and the drummer into electrical signals and feed them to the amplifiers.

Amplifiers. Amplifiers change electrical signals from the guitars, microphones, and keyboard into loud sounds.

Reggae Greats

There are many well-known reggae groups, musicians, producers and sound-system men, and songs. Here are some lists of just a few of the most popular reggae greats.

Musicians

- Jimmy Cliff
- Desmond Dekker
- Bob Marley
- Peter Tosh
- Bunny Wailer

Groups

- Black Uhuru
- Burning Spear
- Culture
- The Mighty Diamonds
- Toots and the Maytals
- The Wailers

Producers and Sound-System Men

- Sir Coxone Dodd
- King Jammy
- Lee "Scratch" Perry
- Prince Buster
- Duke Reid

Songs

- "The Harder They Come," by Jimmy Cliff

- "Israelites," by Desmond Dekker

- "Slavery Days," by Burning Spear

- "Sponji Reggae," by Black Uhuru

- "Trenchtown Rock," by Bob Marley and the Wailers

Record Labels and Recording Studios

A record label is a company that signs, or hires, bands and then records and sells their music. The term *record label* comes from the paper labels that are pasted in the center of vinyl records. These are some important reggae record labels and some of the artists they have signed.

- Island Records - recorded and released the Wailers' album "Catch A Fire"

- Virgin Records - released a record by the Mighty Diamonds

- Tuff Gong Records - created by Bob Marley, it is one of the largest recording studios in the Caribbean

- Trojan Records - released records by Toots and the Maytals, Lee Perry, and Desmond Dekker

Music Production

The way music is recorded makes a big difference in its final sound. The type of microphone used and where it is placed are very important. The **acoustics** in the recording room are critical.

Recording music is a difficult process. That is why most reggae bands record in recording studios. A recording studio has professional recording equipment.

It also has soundproof rooms. Studio engineers place the microphones and run the equipment.

Once the music is recorded, it needs to be worked with to bring out the best sound. This is mostly done with computer programs that help separate the sounds. This process is called mixing.

This sound engineer is using a mixing board.

Downloading Music

At one time, music could be bought only at record stores. Today you can buy music by downloading it onto your computer from a Web site. You can then put the downloaded music onto an MP3 player.

Sometimes people violate **copyright** law when they download music. Copyright law helps musicians get paid for their music. Some illegal Web sites let people download music without paying. You need to make sure you are downloading music from a legal Web site. Otherwise, you could be breaking copyright law.

It is also important that you get permission from an adult before downloading music. When you download music, you are charged a fee. Make sure an adult knows how much the music costs. And make sure an adult knows the Web site you are downloading from.

Record Collecting

Many people collect vinyl records. Music stores sell new and used records. You can also find used records at garage and estate sales. Many **audiophiles** prefer the sound of records. They believe the sound is warmer and truer than the sound of CDs.

Dancehall DJs play records of dub music on two **turntables** and blend the music between songs. This continues the beat through many different songs. And, it makes the music very easy to dance to.

There are many ways to listen to reggae music. You can go to a live performance or listen to the radio. You can check out music at your local library or go to a community center or a museum.

At many libraries, you can check out CDs and DVDs for free. You can watch concerts on DVDs, cable channels, and public television. Here are just a few ways you can experience and learn about reggae music.

Local Concert Venues

Local newspapers usually list concerts. Look in the entertainment section for upcoming concerts. If you are under 18, the **venue** may require that you attend with an adult. Reggae bands play at stadiums, state fairs, park bandstands, art and music festivals, and theaters.

Community Centers and Museums

Community centers are great places to learn about reggae music. They often have classes that teach dance and music. Some host performances of live reggae music.

Some Jamaican museums tell the history of reggae music. Some U.S. museums host traveling exhibits about reggae music. Check your local newspaper for reggae music exhibits visiting your hometown. Or visit one of these famous reggae music centers or museums.

Ashkenaz Music & Dance Community Center

Berkeley, CA
www.ashkenaz.com

This community center focuses on world and **roots music**. It offers dance classes, live performances, and special concerts for kids.

WorldBeat Cultural Center

San Diego, CA
www.worldbeatcenter.org

This cultural organization is dedicated to world music. It holds annual festivals celebrating reggae music and musicians.

Bob Marley Museum

Kingston, Jamaica
www.bobmarley-foundation.com/museum.html

This museum contains photographs, **memorabilia**, and writings about the life and music of Bob Marley.

Coffee-Can
BONGOS

Step 1

Using the ruler, measure and mark a spot four inches (10 cm) down from the top of one can. Mark another spot two inches (5 cm) below the first spot. Make sure that the marks are in a straight line. Repeat this on the other coffee can. Make sure that the marks match on both cans.

Step 2

Next, make holes through the marks on both cans. You will need an adult helper for this step. Hold the nail on one of the marks. Hammer the nail so it pierces the can and makes a hole. Repeat this at each mark on the two cans.

Step 3

Now line up the two cans so the holes match. Push the bolts through both sets of holes. Be careful not to cut yourself on the sharp edges.

Step 4

Attach the wing nuts to the bolts. Screw them down tightly to hold the coffee cans together. Attach the plastic lids and your bongos are finished! Try playing them with pencils, chopsticks, or the palms of your hands.

Cool
CLAVES

CLEF NOTES

Claves are a type of musical instrument also known as an idiophone. The whole instrument vibrates to make a sound when it is struck or scraped. Other idiophones include gongs and cymbals.

Step 1

Using the ruler, mark two equal lengths on the piece of wood. You can make your claves one foot (30 cm) long or two feet (61 cm) long, whichever you prefer!

Step 2

Ask an adult helper to cut the wood with the saw. You can help by holding the wood firmly in place.

Step 3

Smooth the cut edges with the sandpaper. You will need to work the sandpaper for some time to make sure the edges are smooth and rounded. You will be playing the claves with your hands, and you won't want to get splinters!

Step 4

Your claves are finished! To play them, grasp one clave lightly with your fingers. Hold the other clave gently in your other hand. Tap the two claves together. Do not hold the claves too tightly or it will affect the sound.

Bamboo
SCRAPER

Step 1

Measure and mark 15 equally spaced marks on the bamboo. Make sure that you leave a space at one end of the bamboo. This is where you will hold the scraper when you play it.

Step 2

Next, use the utility knife to cut a notch on each mark you made. Make sure you have permission from an adult to use the utility knife. Or ask an adult to cut the notches for you. It will take two cuts to make each wedge-shaped notch.

Step 3

Your bamboo scraper is finished. To play it, hold one end with your hand. Scrape a pencil, screwdriver, or dowel across the notches. See which one makes the best sound!

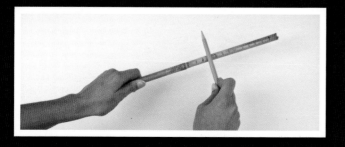

CLEF NOTES

Jamaican folk music uses several kinds of homemade **percussion** instruments. Some people make shakers out of hollow coconut shells filled with dried beans. Others make scrapers out of cheese graters!

Dub Song LYRICS

Create your own reggae song by writing **lyrics** to a dub song. Dub songs are instrumental versions of reggae songs. You can find dub compilation CDs at a music store or at your local library. Find a song you like and then start writing your lyrics! When you are finished, try replacing some of your lyrics with Rasta words from the dictionary on the next page.

Step 1

Pick a story you want to tell. Or write about an emotion or a topic such as peace or love. Think of some main ideas for your song.

Step 2

Next, think of some title ideas. Brainstorm on a piece of notebook paper. Make a list of ideas you want to include in your lyrics. Don't think too much, just let your ideas flow!

Main Idea:

- peace

Title Ideas:

- One Day
- peaceful ways
- The way I Live
- In This world

Lyric Ideas:

- ways to live peacefully
- what peace means to me
- what peace can do for people
- kindness to others

Step 3

Next, start writing! Write your chorus, which is the repeating part of the song. This part usually includes the title of the song. It should also state the main idea of the song.

Step 4

Now write a couple of verses that tell the listener about your story or subject. Try to write with feeling. Remember, music is all about emotion.

Step 5

Finally, sing or chant your lyrics while the dub music plays. Experiment to find the best sound for your lyrics. Then, check the Rasta dictionary. Try to replace as many words as you can with their Rasta **equivalents**.

Have fun singing your new reggae song! Ask someone to videotape your performance. Try playing one of your rhythm makers while singing!

Rasta Dictionary

big up – to praise someone.

braata – a little more, or extra.

dawta – a girl, woman, or sister.

di – the.

dis – this.

diss – to show disrespect.

dread – serious.

ease-up – to forgive.

gi – give.

gravalicious – greedy.

i-man – I, me, mine.

irie – fine or good.

ital – natural, unprocessed food.

laba-laba – to talk.

labrish – gossip.

madda – mother.

natty dread – a Rastafarian with dreadlocks.

one love – an expression of unity.

sata – to rejoice.

seen – understood.

wa mek – why.

youth – a young or immature man.

erials
:ded

e song, such as
chtown Rock" by
Marley or "Reggae
Soul" by Toots and
Maytals

Cool Reggae DANCE

Hey mon, let's dance! Reggae's swinging rhythm and simple chords make it easy to dance to.

Since reggae music is partly based on African music, try some African movements. African dance is used to express feelings and uses all parts of the body. You can make your movements as wild or as calm as you want. These dances are the basics. You can make up your own versions of these moves!

tep 1

ay the reggae song
ou've chosen. Now,
tart the basic step
or the bottom half of
our body. Bend your
torso so you are slightly
hunched forward.

Step 2

Next, start bending
your knees to the
beat. Bend one knee
at a time, alternating
for each beat. Keep
your feet planted on
the ground.

Step 3

Next, work on the top half of your body. Bob your head and shrug your shoulders to the reggae beat. Alternate shrugging each shoulder to the beat. Move your head from side to side. Look down or look up. Do whatever you feel like doing!

Step 4

Now add your arms to the dance. This is where you can really get wild if you want! Every time you shrug your shoulder, add an arm movement on that side. Try keeping your arms bent at the elbow while moving your arms forward. Or try raising each arm all the way, swinging to the music.

CLEF NOTES

Dancing has always been a big part of Jamaican culture. A dance called the Jonkunnu has been around since the time of slavery. In December, Jonkunnu dancers parade through the streets of Jamaican towns and villages. Some dancers wear masks of horse heads and cow heads. Another dancer wears a costume that looks like it is made out of leaves. That character is called Jack in de Green.

Step 5

Put all these movements together, and you'll be grooving to the reggae beat!

Sound-System PARTY

Materials Needed

- CDs
- construction paper
- markers
- portable stereo with a CD player
- extension cord
- portable table

Starting in the early 1950s, many Jamaicans first heard popular songs on sound systems. The term *sound system* meant not just the sound equipment but also the people who played the music. These sound systems were portable dance parties that were held outside. A DJ would play the latest songs on a **turntable**, and huge speakers would blast out the music.

Try putting on your own sound-system party at your home. Remember to ask for permission before you plan your party.

Step 1

First, go to the library and check out as many reggae CDs as you can find.

Step 2

Next, create your own DJ **persona**. Pick a funky name for yourself. Try using a royal title, such as king, queen, prince, or knight. Shorten your last name or make up a nickname for yourself. Put the two names together and that will be your DJ name.

Step 3

Now, create a flyer and a sign for your sound-system party. Use the Rasta colors of red, green, and gold. Title the flyer and use your DJ name. Write the time and the date on the flyer. Give a copy of the flyer to everyone you want to invite to the party. Make a sign to hang by your sound system.

Step 5

When your guests arrive, start playing the music. Make sure you always have another song ready to play. This way, there will always be a reggae song pumping out of your sound system!

Step 4

Set up your sound system in your backyard. Put the portable table outside. Set your stereo on the table. Connect the extension cord to the stereo and plug it into an outlet in your house. Hang your sign on the table.

CLEF NOTES

Sound-system DJs would often compete with each other. Duke Reid and Sir Coxone Dodd were the two biggest sound-system men in Jamaica during the 1950s and 1960s. The crowds were extremely loyal to their favorite DJs.

Conclusion

It's hard to believe that a sound heard around the world came from a small Caribbean island. But, Jamaica's reggae music is celebrated and loved by many.

Reggae music now flavors many other **genres** with its unique sound. In all parts of the world, you can hear local bands play their own versions of this upbeat music. You can hear rock songs with a reggae beat. You can hear punk songs with a ska sound. Reggae's musical influence can be heard in many ways.

Study songs by the musicians who invented this special sound. Create a CD collection of your reggae favorites. As you listen to reggae, ska, and rock steady music, note your favorite elements of the music. Then, as you play your own music, inject a few of these elements into your songs. Experiment and create your own reggae style.

You can definitely have fun with reggae music, whether you dance, play, or listen to it!

Glossary

acoustics – the properties of a room that affect how sound is heard in it.

audiophile – a person who is very enthusiastic about listening to recorded music.

copyright – the legal right to copy, sell, publish, or distribute the work of a writer, musician, or artist.

dreadlock – a hairstyle in which the hair is twisted into thick, ropelike strands.

equivalent – being the same as or equal to another.

genre – a category of art, music, or literature.

jazz – a style of music characterized by complex rhythms and melodies and improvised solos.

lyrics – the words of a song.

memorabilia – items that serve as a remembrance of a person or an event.

percussion – an instrument played by hitting, shaking, or striking it.

persona – a made-up character or personality.

Rastafarianism – a religious movement that originated in Jamaica in the 1930s. It teaches that Ethiopia is the promised land and former emperor Haile Selassie is a god.

rhythm and blues – a style of music that has roots in African-American folk music and blues. It is characterized by a strong back beat and simple chords.

riff – a simple musical phrase that is repeated to form the basis of a song.

roots music – a style of traditional music linked to a certain place or a particular ethnic culture.

turntable – the round, rotating platform on which records are placed; a record player.

venue – a place where specific kinds of events take place.

Web Sites

To learn more about cool music, visit ABDO Publishing Company on the World Wide Web at **www.abdopublishing.com**. Web sites about cool music are featured on our Book Links pages. These links are routinely monitored and updated to provide the most current information available.

Index